ANIMAL STATS

DINOSAURS

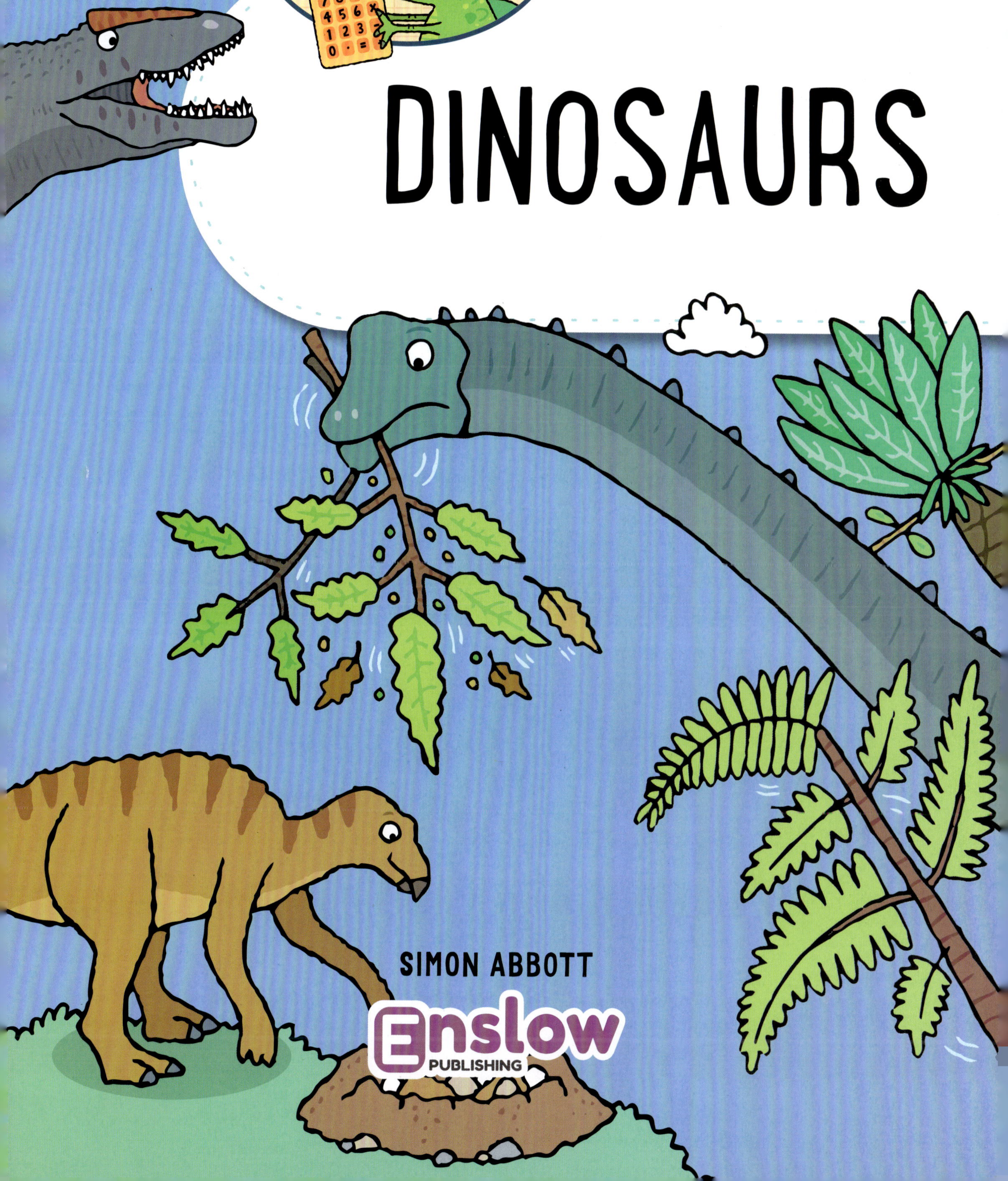

SIMON ABBOTT

Enslow PUBLISHING

Published in 2027 by Enslow Publishing, LLC
2544 Clinton Street
Buffalo, NY 14224

First published in Great Britain in 2025 by Wayland

Printed in China

CPSIA compliance information: Batch #QS27ENS: For further information contact Enslow Publishing LLC, New York, New York at 1-800-398-2504.

Please visit our website, www.enslowpublishing.com. For a free color catalog of all our high-quality books, call toll free 1-800-398-2504 or fax 1-877-980-4454.

Cataloging-in-Publication Data

Names: Abbott, Simon, 1967-.
Title: Dinosaurs / Simon Abbott.
Description: Buffalo, NY : Enslow Publishing, 2027. |
Series: Animal stats | Includes glossary.
Identifiers: ISBN 9781978549326 (pbk.) | ISBN 9781978549333 (library bound) |
ISBN 9781978549340 (ebook)
Subjects: LCSH: Dinosaurs--Juvenile literature.
Classification: LCC QE861.5 A34 2027 | DDC 567.9--dc23

CONTENTS

ARE YOU PREPARED FOR THE TRIP OF A LIFETIME?

Let's travel back **245 million** years and get familiar with some extraordinary creatures from the past – the dinosaurs!

We'll get up close with dinos as heavy as **20** hippos and flying reptiles with a wingspan as wide as a fighter jet!

Our expedition will reveal why these magnificent creatures no longer roam our planet, and which dinosaurs are ancestors of the birds we see flying around today.

SO SIT BACK, RELAX, AND GET READY FOR

AN ADVENTURE SPANNING OVER

160 MILLION YEARS!

PREHISTORIC PREPARATION

Dinosaurs first stomped around on Earth around **245 million** years ago. These spectacular creatures dominated our planet for over **160 million** years, until they eventually became extinct around **65 million** years ago.

Take a look at the timeline!

Era	Period	Time		
Mesozoic Era	TRIASSIC	245 million years ago	Dinosaurs	
	JURASSIC	201 million years ago	Dinosaurs	
	CRETACEOUS	145 million years ago	Dinosaurs	
Cenozoic Era	PALEOGENE	66 million years ago	Early horses	
	NEOGENE	23 million years ago	Early camels	
	QUATERNARY	2.5 million years ago	Early apes	

245 million years ago, Earth was one massive continent known as **Pangea**, surrounded by a vast ocean named **Panthalassa**.

Over time, this landmass broke apart and drifted to form the familiar continents we know today.

Hard to believe? Well, in fact, the continents have joined together and spread apart at least **three times** before. After all, our planet is **4.5 billion** years old, so on that time scale, **200+ million** years ago isn't such a long time!

Geologists have found identical rocks on different continents that were formed before the continents split apart. These rocks contain the same minerals and were created under the same conditions.

Fossils of the Mesosaurus dinosaur species have been discovered in both South America and Africa. These dinosaurs lived on Earth before the two continents separated. In fact, dinosaur fossils have been found on every continent, even Antarctica!

Before dinosaurs appeared, Earth went through a disastrous environmental event called the **Permian-Triassic extinction**, or the "Great Dying."

90% of all species were wiped out, and it took **10 million** years for the planet to recover. Less than **5%** of marine life survived, while only a third of large animals on land pulled through. It would take an additional **14 million** years for coral reefs to begin rebuilding.

So, what caused this catastrophic emergency on Earth? Well, scientists are still looking at the evidence – after all, this did happen over **250 million** years ago!

The leading theory is that volcanic eruptions released a huge amount of carbon dioxide and other greenhouse gases into the atmosphere. This resulted in intense heat, causing coal beds to ignite, showering ash and debris into the sky.

As a result, the sun was blotted out triggering global warming, and oxygen levels in both the air and oceans were greatly reduced.

FUNGI FACT

Scientists believe that the winner in the Permian-Triassic wipeout was fungi!

Microscopic organisms called **reduviasporonites** emerged and exploded around the planet, making their home inside the **billions** of dead and rotting trees covering Earth's devastated forests.

Researchers call this a **fungal spike!**

How did this event lead to the "reptile rule" and dinosaur dominance of the Triassic period? Some scientists argue that their incredible speed gave them a competitive advantage, while others put it down to their wide range of physical adaptations. (We'll be looking at their huge claws, sails, beaks, tails, and supersharp teeth later!)

Another theory could be their unusual breathing system. It is thought that dinosaurs had super-efficient, bird-like lungs, which allowed them to take in **60–65%** of the oxygen breathed, (compared to your **20–25%**). That put dinosaurs in pole position in the low-oxygen conditions following the Permian-Triassic extinction.

DINO DOSSIER

Let's take a moment to get familiar with some **E.D.I.'s** - that's **Essential Dinosaur Information!**

What does "dinosaur" mean?

It comes from two Greek words: deinos (meaning terrible) and saurus (meaning lizard). The term was coined by Richard Owen, the first director of London's Natural History Museum, in 1842. After years of studying fossils, he needed a new classification for these creatures that were different from modern-day lizards.

How was each dinosaur named?

Typically, the names are a combination of Greek and Latin words that describe the dinosaur's characteristics or behaviors. Some names also honor a person or include the location where the fossilized remains were discovered.

Here are some examples:

OVIRAPTOR		Meaning: **EGG THIEF**
SEISMOSAURUS		Meaning: **EARTH-SHAKING LIZARD**
TRICERATOPS		Meaning: **THREE-HORNED FACE**

In the past, scientists were baffled by the discovery of fossils due to their lack of understanding about evolution, extinction, and Earth's history. Before the development of **paleontology** (the study of ancient life), the identification of prehistoric bones was a guessing game.

Theories included a range of mythical creatures such as unicorns, sea serpents, dragons, giants, and cyclopes!

How many species of dinosaur are there?

There are around **700** known species of extinct dinosaurs.

They can be divided into two groups, based on the arrangement of their hip bones:

1 - SAURISCHIANS

(Have pelvic hips like lizards)

THEROPODS

The only meat-eating dinosaurs.

Walked on **two** powerful legs, with short arms and sharp claws.

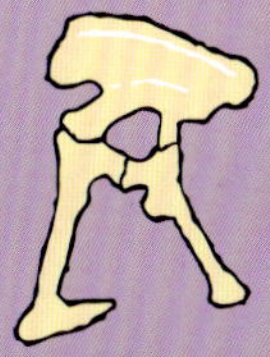

SAURISCHIAN HIP BONE

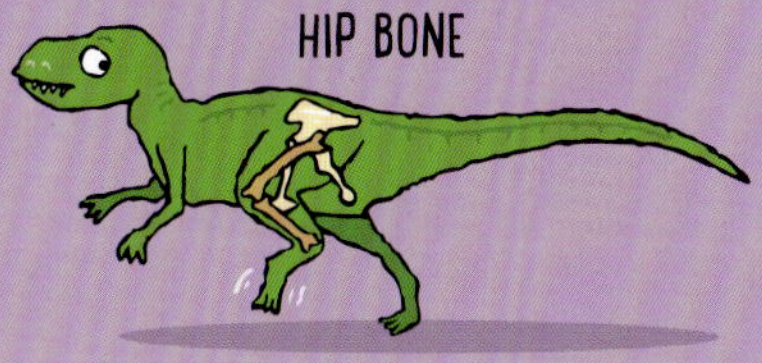

SAUROPODS

Large plant-eating dinosaurs, or herbivores.

Walked on all **four** feet, had small heads and long tails and neck for reaching the highest branches.

2 - ORNITHISCHIANS

(Have hip bones more like birds)

THYREOPHORA

Includes:

Stegosaurs

(meaning plated or roofed reptile)

Slow-moving dinosaurs who walked on all **fours**.

Their bodies were covered in bony plates or spikes.

Ankylosauria

(meaning armor-covered or fused together reptile)

Small to medium dinosaurs, covered in flexible body armor.

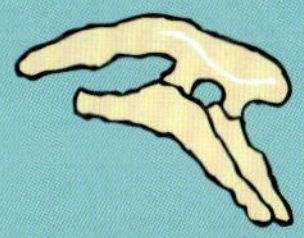

ORNITHISCHIAN HIP BONE

CERAPODS

Includes:

Ceratopsia

(meaning horned-faced reptile)

Most had horned or frilled heads or superstrong beaks.

Ornithopoda

(meaning bird feet)

These dinosaurs walked and ran on two back feet.

Pachycephalosauria

(meaning thick-headed lizard)

Thick-skulled dinosaurs that moved slowly on their back legs.

TRIASSIC TIMES

Get ready ... the dinosaurs are on their way! Let's set the scene for their arrival. What did life on Earth look like in the Triassic period?

WHEN: 252-201 million years ago

LANDMASS: Pangea

CLIMATE: Warm and dry, with seasonal monsoons.

ANIMALS: The first dinosaurs roamed the land.
Reptiles grew in diversity.
Spiders, scorpions, millipedes, and centipedes that had survived the Permian extinction.
The first mammal, a specimen about 4 inches long (10 cm) called a ***morganucodon***, appeared. The oceans were packed with coiled-shelled **ammonites**, **mollusks**, and **sea urchins**.

PLANT LIFE: Conifers, ginkgoes, and seed ferns flourished.

THE TROPICAL TRIASSIC!

Temperatures on Earth soared to record levels during the start of the Triassic period. The ocean's surface heated up to **104°F** (40°C) compared to today's average of **62.6°F** (17°C), while land temperatures climbed as high as **140°F** (60°C) significantly higher than the current average of **59°F** (15°C).

Who were the stand-out **Triassic** dinosaurs? Let's take a look:

EORAPTOR

MEANING: Early or dawn plunderer

LENGTH: **5.5 ft** (1.7 m)

WEIGHT: **22 lb** (10 kg) like a dachshund

FOSSILS FOUND IN: Argentina

DIET:

Omnivore (it ate plants and animals)
Its top teeth were long, sharp, and jagged for cutting meat and the bottom teeth were blunt for chomping on tough vegetation.

FACT FILE:

Eoraptor is one of the oldest dinosaurs ever found and lived roughly **228 million** years ago.

COELOPHYSIS

MEANING: Hollow form

LENGTH: **6.5 ft** (2 m) imagine **3** tennis rackets end-to-end

WEIGHT: **60 lb** (27 kg)

FOSSILS FOUND IN: US, Zimbabwe, and China

DIET:

Carnivore (it ate other animals)
Its teeth were small and razor-sharp.

FACT FILE:

Coelophysis was aptly named for its hollow limb bones, which made it a swift and nimble predator.

PLATEOSAURUS

MEANING: Flat lizard

LENGTH: **23 ft** (7 m) (or two-and-a-half times the length of your bed!)

WEIGHT: **8,800 lb** (4,000 kg)

FOSSILS FOUND IN: Germany and Greenland

DIET:
Herbivore (it ate plants)
It had grinding teeth and a hard, horny beak.

FACT FILE:
Plateosaurus had **five** fingers and a large thumb claw, to forage for food or defend itself.

MUSSAURUS

MEANING: Mouse lizard

LENGTH: **10 ft** (3 m)

WEIGHT: At birth, this dinosaur was the size of your hand, but as an adult it weighed over a ton!

FOSSILS FOUND IN: Argentina

DIET:
Herbivore (it ate plants)
Mussaurus constantly grew new teeth to replace the ones worn down by chewing through Triassic plants.

FACT FILE:
This dinosaur moved around on **four** legs when it was first born, then switched to **two** legs as it grew up – just like humans. We know that ***Mussaurus*** were social dinosaurs, as **100** eggs and bones from **80** individual creatures were found in the same location.

COLORADISAURUS

MEANING: Los Colorados lizard
LENGTH: **13 ft** (4 m)
WEIGHT: **1,300 lb** (600 kg)
(the same as 4 pandas)
FOSSILS FOUND IN: Argentina

DIET:
Omnivore (it ate plants and animals)
It walked on **four** legs, but stood on its rear legs to feed on leaves from high branches.

FACT FILE:
This dinosaur's skull was discovered by paleontologist Jose F. Bonaparte in Argentina. He originally named this specimen ***Coloradia***, but had to think again as that name was taken by a moth!

STAURIKOSAURUS

MEANING: Southern Cross lizard
LENGTH: **6.5 ft** (2 m)
WEIGHT: **65 lb** (30 kg)
(or a third of a kangaroo!)
FOSSILS FOUND IN: Brazil

DIET:
Carnivore (it ate other animals)
This dinosaur had sharp, curved teeth and a powerful bite. It is likely that ***Staurikosaurus*** was a predator of small vertebrates and scavenged the kills of larger dinosaurs.

FACT FILE:
This sleek therapod had a long tail with over **40** vertebrae, which would have helped it to balance when running.

JURASSIC GENERATION

Time is moving on. What major changes took place in the Jurassic period, and which new dinosaurs were dominating the landscape?

WHEN: 201-145 million years ago

LANDMASS: Pangea splits apart into two landmasses: Laurasia (Northern region) and Gondwana (Southern region).

CLIMATE: Warm summers and cold, dark winters.
Oceans were around 14°F (8°C) warmer than the present day.

ANIMALS: Birds made their first appearance.
A diverse ocean life, with thriving reefs, large marine predators, and shallow water invertebrates.
Insects included the **giant lacewing** with a 2-inch (5 cm) wingspan - double the size of lacewings today!

PLANT LIFE: Horsetails, cycads, and cypress trees.

The end of the Triassic period was marked by the fourth major mass extinction event to impact our planet. Over a span of 18 million years, 76% of all species on land and in the sea were wiped out, making way for dinosaurs to become the dominant land creatures on Earth.

Here come the Jurassic dinosaurs. Let's check them out:

MEGALOSAURUS

MEANING: Big lizard

LENGTH: **20 ft** (6 m)
(half the length of a *T rex*)

WEIGHT: **3,300 lb** (1,500 kg)
(the same as two average cows!)

FOSSILS FOUND IN: England

DIET:
Carnivore (it ate other animals)

FACT FILE:
When these fossils were found nobody knew what a dinosaur was! In 1824, ***Megalosaurus*** became the **first** dinosaur in history to be given a name (remember, this was **18** years before the word was invented).

COMPSOGNATHUS

MEANING: Pretty jaw

LENGTH: **25.5 in** (65 cm)

WEIGHT: **6.5 lb** (3 kg)
(or twice the weight of a human brain)

FOSSILS FOUND IN: France and Germany

DIET:
Carnivore (it ate other animals)
Small, speedy lizards have been found in the bellies of this dinosaur's remains.

FACT FILE:
This chicken-sized specimen is one of the smallest dinosaurs. It had **two** long legs, **three-toed** feet, small, sharp teeth, and a long tail for balance and stability.

STEGOSAURUS

DIET:
Herbivore (it ate plants)
It ate small stones called **gastroliths** to help break up the tough plant material in its stomach.

MEANING: Roof lizard
LENGTH: **29.5 ft** (9 m)
(twice the length of a hippo, with a brain the size of a plum!)
WEIGHT: **3,500 lb** (1,600 kg)
FOSSILS FOUND IN: US

FACT FILE:
The bony plates down its back were attached to its skin, not its skeleton. Scientists aren't **100%** sure what these plates were used for: to warn off predators, regulate body heat, or to recognize members of the same species?

GARGOYLEOSAURUS

DIET:
Herbivore (it ate plants)

MEANING: Gargoyle lizard
LENGTH: **13 ft** (4 m)
(imagine two Christmas trees laid end-to-end)
WEIGHT: Up to **2,200 lb** (1,000 kg)
FOSSILS FOUND IN: US

FACT FILE:
Gargoyleosaurus is one of the oldest **ankylosaurs** discovered. Its "armor" included horns on the back of its head, shoulder spines, a pelvic shield, and bony plates running down its tail.

DIPLODOCUS

MEANING: Double beam

LENGTH: **85 ft** (26 m) and almost as tall as a giraffe

WEIGHT: **33,000 lb** (15,000 kg) (the equivalent to eight giraffes)

FOSSILS FOUND IN: US

DIET:

Herbivore (it ate plants)

Diplodocus had a **21-foot-long** (6.5 m) neck that it raised to reach high vegetation.

FACT FILE:

It's thought that ***Diplodocus***'s record-breaking **43-foot-long** (13 m) tail had two purposes – to counterbalance its neck and act as a ferocious whip to keep predators at bay.

SINRAPTOR

MEANING: Chinese plunderer

LENGTH: **25 ft** (7.6 m) (around the height of an African elephant)

WEIGHT: **2,650 lb** (1,200 kg)

FOSSILS FOUND IN: China

DIET:

Carnivore (it ate other animals)

It most likely hunted juvenile herbivore dinosaurs, inflicting fatal wounds with its razor-like serrated teeth.

FACT FILE:

This apex predator had a bite-force comparable to today's great white shark. With its weight, speed, muscular forearms, and powerful jaw loaded with supersharp teeth, ***Sinraptor*** was, without doubt, a champion hunter.

GUANLONG

DIET:
Carnivore (it ate other animals)

FEATURES:
Guanlong is best known for its distinctive head crest. It was **2.4 inches** (6 cm) and ran along its snout from its nostrils to its eye sockets. It was as thin as a tortilla.

MEANING: Crowned dragon
LENGTH: **10 ft** (3 m) (about one-and-a-half times the height of your front door!)
WEIGHT: **275 lb** (125 kg)
FOSSILS FOUND IN: China

FACT FILE:
To date, **two** have been discovered in the same location. Both died in the same way – they fell into the huge, muddy footprint left by a gigantic herbivore, and they couldn't get out!

KENTROSAURUS

DIET:
Herbivore (it ate plants)
Its beak was toothless, but it did have an assortment of cheek teeth to munch on a mix of plants and shrubs.

MEANING: Spiky lizard
LENGTH: **16.5 ft** (5 m)
WEIGHT: **3,500 lb** (1,600 kg) (the weight of an average car)
FOSSILS FOUND IN: Tanzania

FACT FILE:
The plates down ***Kentrosaurus***'s back merged into spikes on its hip and tail. This could be a powerful weapon of defense, and it's thought that its tail could swing at **80 miles per hour** (130 km/h)!

SCELIDOSAURUS

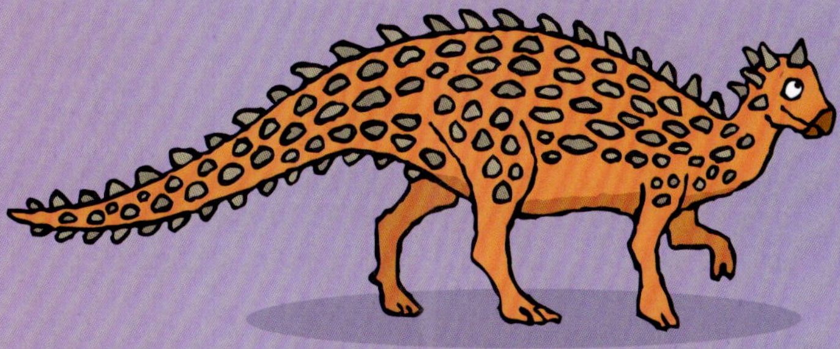

MEANING: Limb lizard

LENGTH: **13 ft** (4 m)
(with a tiny head shorter than the width of this book!)

WEIGHT: **600 lb** (270 kg)
(half the weight of a polar bear)

FOSSILS FOUND IN: UK

DIET:
Herbivore (it ate plants)
Scelidosaurus ate low-lying plants, probably with the addition of fruits and seaweed too.

FACT FILE:
Scelidosaurus was the first complete dinosaur ever identified. Quarry owner James Harrison found the first remains over **170 years** ago and sent them off to paleontologist Richard Owen for identification.

DILOPHOSAURUS

MEANING: Double crested lizard

LENGTH: **20 ft** (6 m)

WEIGHT: **660 lb** (300 kg)

FOSSILS FOUND IN: US

DIET:
Carnivore (it ate other animals)
Dilophosaurus was one of the fiercest predators of its time. It had a gap, or kink, in its upper jaw, which may have been used to grip its prey. Crocodiles today have a similar feature.

FACT FILE:
Paleontologists believe that ***Dilophosaurus'*** crest was brightly colored, to show off to a potential mate. The crest was made of thin bone and may have been covered in **keratin** (the same material that your finger and toenails are made from).

CRETACEOUS COUNTDOWN

Join us as we hop over the boundary from the Jurassic to the Cretaceous period. How would Earth look if we stepped back 145 million years?

WHEN: **145-66 million** years ago

LANDMASS: By the end of the Cretaceous period, the continents shifted into the positions you'd see on a map today.

CLIMATE: Warm temperatures with little or no ice at the North and South Poles.

ANIMALS: On land, anything bigger than **3.3 feet** (1 m) was a dinosaur. Birds had evolved, and large marine reptiles called mosasaurs thrived in the warm ocean. Pollinating bees came on the scene, not long after the first flowering plants appeared.

PLANT LIFE: Polar forests were dominated by conifers, which survived for four months of the year in total darkness. Angiosperms (flowering plants) were an important part of the landscape in the Cretaceous period.

SHIFTING TIMES

There was no major mass extinction event between the Jurassic and Cretaceous periods.

The ecological changes during this era were complex: the global climate shifted from dry to wet, and there is evidence of major asteroid impacts and massive volcanic eruptions.

Let's unearth some amazing dinosaurs from this time:

TRICERATOPS

MEANING: Three-horned face

LENGTH: **29.5 ft** (9 m)
(twice the length of a crocodile)

WEIGHT: **12,000 lb** (5,500 kg)

FOSSILS FOUND IN: US

DIET:
Herbivore (it ate plants)

Triceratops had up to **800** teeth, arranged in vertical stacks. As old teeth wore out, new ones would be pushed to the top.

FACT FILE:
This dinosaur's frill may have helped to protect its neck from the jaws of an attacking predator. It could also have been used as a way to attract potential mates.

ARGENTINOSAURUS

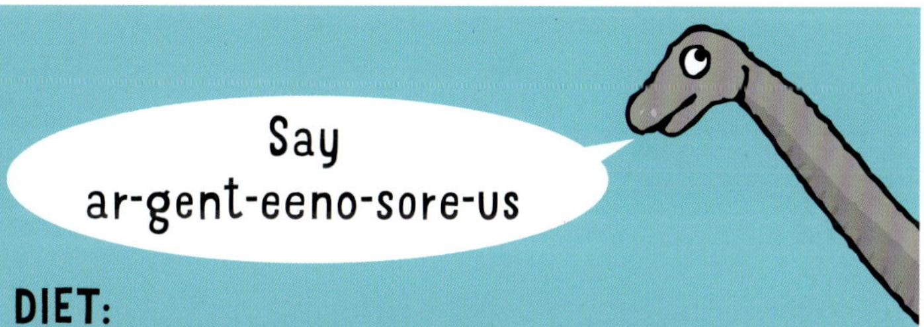

MEANING: Argentina lizard

LENGTH: **115 ft** (35 m)
(about the length of **four** fire engines end-to-end)

WEIGHT: **154,000 lb** (70,000 kg)
(possibly the largest plant-eating dinosaur, but still not as heavy as a blue whale!)

FOSSILS FOUND IN: Argentina

DIET:
Herbivore (it ate plants)
It stripped vegetation from the tallest trees, and munched through around **1,200 pounds** (550 kg) of plant life every day.

FACT FILE:
The first ***Argentinosaurus*** fossil to be found was a vertebrae, or back bone. It measured an amazing **62 inches** (159 cm) – the average human vertebrae measures just over **0.8 inch** (2 cm)!

VELOCIRAPTOR

MEANING: Quick thief

LENGTH: **6 ft** (1.8 m)
(and as tall as a turkey)

WEIGHT: **15 lb** (7 kg)
(the equivalent to three chihuahuas)

FOSSILS FOUND IN: Mongolia

DIET:

Carnivore (it ate other animals)
These predators would sprint toward prey at **25 miles per hour** (40 km/h). ***Velociraptor's*** secret weapon was the **3-inch-long** (8 cm) claws on the second toe of each foot.

FACT FILE:

Scientists believe that this was a feathered dinosaur. So, could it fly? Well, no. More than likely, the feathers were there to preserve body heat, or to dazzle a potential mate!

EDMONTOSAURUS

MEANING: Edmonton lizard (after the location where it was discovered)

LENGTH: **43 ft** (13 m)

WEIGHT: **7,500 lb** (3,400 kg)
(almost as heavy as a hippo!)

FOSSILS FOUND IN: Canada

DIET:

Herbivore (it ate plants)
Hard conifer needles, twigs, and seeds were found in the stomachs of ***Edmontosaurus*** remains. This dinosaur had over **1,000** teeth, set in rows and columns.

FACT FILE:

A baby ***Edmontosaurus*** weighed around the same as a human baby, even though they were **twice** as long. That's because **half** the baby dinosaur was made up of a long, light tail.

TROODON

MEANING: Wounding tooth

LENGTH: **6.5 ft** (2 m)

WEIGHT: **90 lb** (40 kg)

(with a brain the size of a golf ball, it had the biggest brain-to-body ratio of any dinosaur we know of.)

FOSSILS FOUND IN: US

DIET:

Carnivore (it ate other animals)

A large brain equates to exceptional eyesight, heightened hearing, and a superior sense of smell - all great traits for a predatory dinosaur. ***Troodon*** possessed large, front-facing eyes, which could have enabled it to hunt at night as well.

FACT FILE:

This dinosaur's large brain and nesting behavior suggests that ***Troodon*** could be the vital evolutionary link between its crocodilian ancestors and its later bird relatives.

ANKYLOSAURUS

MEANING: Fused lizard

LENGTH: **26 ft** (8 m)

WEIGHT: **17,600 lb** (8,000 kg)

(or **twice** the weight of a hippo)

FOSSILS FOUND IN: US

DIET:

Herbivore (it ate plants)

This dinosaur chomped down plant material equivalent in weight to **500** bananas every single day.

FACT FILE:

Ankylosaurus was covered with an armored layer of bony plates under a protective layer of keratin. These defensive bones were even found in its eyelids!

TYRANNOSAURUS REX

> Say
> tie-ran-oh-sore-us recks

MEANING: Tyrant lizard

LENGTH: **39 ft** (12 m) (around the length of a bus)

WEIGHT: **15,400 lb** (7,000 kg)

FOSSILS FOUND IN: Canada

DIET:

Carnivore (it ate other animals)

With **60** razor-sharp teeth, each measuring **8 inches** (20 cm) long, and a bone-crunching bite three times stronger than a lion, ***Tyrannosaurus rex*** was one of the most terrifying creatures of all time.

FACT FILE:

A large portion of ***T rex's*** brain was devoted to smell – it had as many "smell cells," or olfactory receptors as a domestic cat. But these hunters weren'tspeedy! Experts have worked out that ***Tyrannosaurus rex*** could only jog at **12 miles per hour** (19 km/h).

PARASAUROLOPHUS

MEANING: Near crested lizard

LENGTH: **29.5 ft** (9 m)

WEIGHT: **11,000 lb** (5,000 kg) (the equivalent of two-and-a-half rhinoceroses)

FOSSILS FOUND IN: Canada

> Say
> pa-ra-sore-ol-off-us

DIET:

Herbivore (it ate plants)

FACT FILE:

The ***Parasaurolophus*** is famous for its extraordinary **5-foot-long** (1.5 m) head crest. A clever paleontologist studied the arrangement of tubes inside the crest. He recreated the structure using plastic tubing, blew through it, and out came a loud and low foghorn-like bellow. It's not certain what ***Parasaurolophus*** used this sound for.

OVIRAPTOR

MEANING: Egg thief
LENGTH: **6.5 ft** (2 m)
WEIGHT: **80 lb** (36 kg)
(about the same as a dalmatian)
FOSSILS FOUND IN: Mongolia

DIET:
Carnivore (it ate other animals)
This dinosaur probably survived on mollusks and crustaceans that it cracked open with its toothless beak.

FACT FILE:
Don't get confused by this dinosaur's "egg thief" name. The fact is, the ***oviraptor*** brooded and guarded its eggs, in a similar way to birds.

GIGANTORAPTOR

MEANING: Giant thief
LENGTH: **26 ft** (8 m)
(the largest known beaked dinosaur)
WEIGHT: **4,400 lb** (2,000 kg)
(that's heavier than a giraffe)
FOSSILS FOUND IN: Mongolia

DIET:
Gigantoraptor was toothless, with a small head and long neck, which points to it being a plant eater. However, it had supersharp claws, which suggests a meat eater! It probably ate both plants and meat.

FACT FILE:
Gigantoraptor was discovered on camera! A TV crew was making a documentary about the paleontologist Xu Xing, and asked if they could film him excavating a sauropod bone for their video. As the fossil was revealed, Xu was astonished – it wasn't a sauropod after all, but the remains of an undiscovered gigantic theropod!

WHEN IT COMES TO THE CRUNCH

Let's serve up some data about a dinosaur's diet. How did these colossal creatures keep their energy levels high?

When it comes to prehistoric nourishment, dinosaurs can be split into three main groups:

HERBIVORES:
Those that primarily ate plant material, such as ***Archaeoceratops***.

CARNIIVORES:
Those that mainly consumed other animals, like ***Allosaurus***.

OMNIVORES:
Those that had a mixed diet of both plants and animals, for example ***Gigantoraptor***.

FISHY FACTS

Recent research suggests ***Spinosaurus***, though **60 feet** (18 m) long, may have been able to hunt fish in water. It had a heavy bone structure, a wide, paddle-like tail and blade-like claws **6.5 inches long** (16.5 cm), which were ideal for propelling itself through the water to capture slippery fish!

DAILY DIET

It is estimated that an adult ***T. rex*** required the same daily calories as **80** humans.

That works out to **300 POUNDS** (140 kg) of meat— around **43** chickens — every day!

GIGANOTOSAURUS TEETH

One way to determine what type of food a dinosaur ate is by studying its teeth. Meat-eating dinosaurs typically had long, sharp, and curved teeth, with powerful jaws to grab and tear their prey.

Giganotosaurus, for instance, had **76** knife-like teeth each measuring **8 inches** (20 cm) long. Its skull was almost the length of your bed, and it could reach speeds of up to **30 miles per hour** (50 km/h) while chasing its prey.

Scientists believe that this predatory dinosaur hunted large herbivorous dinosaurs and have even found evidence of an ***Argentinosaurus*** stuck between its teeth!

A plant-eating dinosaur was equipped with wide, flat, ridged teeth to mash and grind through vegetation. As these teeth were worn down, new ones replaced them. It's thought that ***Diplodocus*** grew a brand new tooth every **35** days!

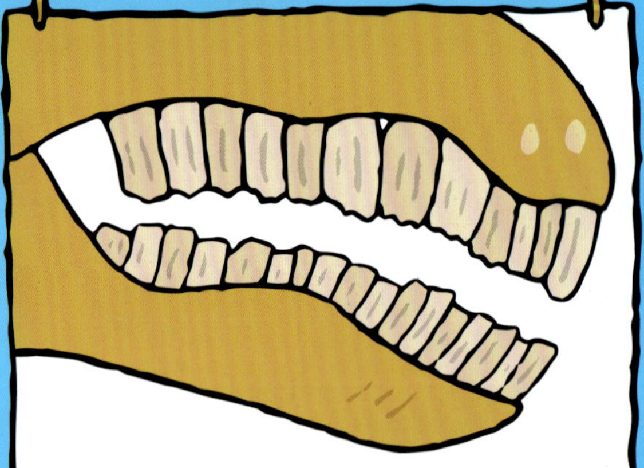

DIPLODOCUS TEETH

STEGOSAURUS TEETH

Some herbivores had up to **nine** baby teeth in each socket, ready to pop up and take the old one's place. ***Stegosaurus*** had around **78** small, flat triangular teeth, which it used to grind down moss, ferns, horsetails, cycads, conifers, and fruit.

In addition to their grating teeth, many plant-eating dinosaurs developed incredibly long necks to reach the leaves and twigs of super-tall trees.

Mamenchisaurus sinocanadorum is estimated to have had a neck length of **50 feet** (15 m) - over **8 times** longer than a giraffe's neck!

To support such a long neck, scans have revealed that the dinosaur's neck bones were filled with air pockets. This is similar to structures found in the necks of modern-day birds, such as storks and swans.

STONE COLD STATISTICS

Many of these herbivore dinosaurs would swallow stones called **gastroliths** to help grind up their food with their powerful stomach muscles. This process is still common today among crocodiles, seals, sea lions, and plant-eating birds. Prehistoric gastroliths could be as long as **4 inches** (10 cm).

When it comes to a dinosaur's diet, we can study teeth, claws, gastroliths – and poo!

Fossilized feces are called **coprolites**, and can come in all shapes and sizes, from a **few inches** to over **24 inches** (60 cm).

The shape of the poo can give insight into the type of animal it came from; for example, a prehistoric shark with spiral-shaped intestines would leave behind spiral-shaped droppings.

PREHISTORIC POO PIONEER

When it comes to coprolite discoveries we have famous fossil-hunter Mary Anning to thank.

Over **200** years ago, Mary became the first person to look inside these fossils and uncover the remains of bones, scales, and fish. Today, her groundbreaking work can be seen on display in London's Natural History Museum.

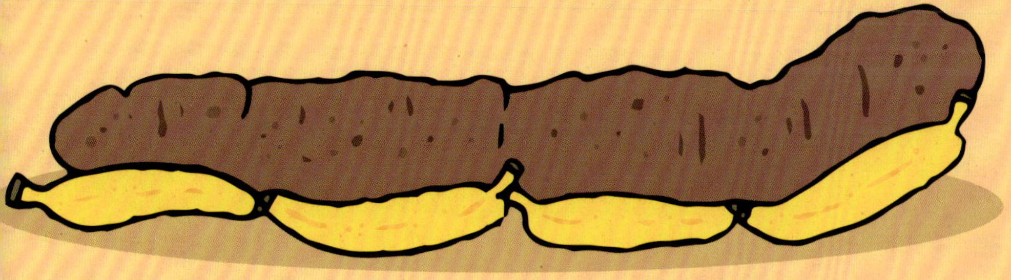

The largest coprolite from a meat-eating dinosaur found weighs **20.5 pounds** (9.3 kg) and measures **26.6 inches** (67.5 cm) long – that's the length of **four** bananas.

When it comes to herbivores, scientists have calculated that an ***Argentinosaurus*** would generate about **880 POUNDS** (400 kg) of poo each day. That's the equivalent of **60** watermelons!

EGG-CITING NEWS!

As far as we know, all dinosaurs arrived on Earth in the same way – they hatched from eggs. Let's eggs-plore the facts and figures!

Fossil evidence has shown that some dinosaurs developed an "**egg tooth**," which they used to break open the tough shell when it was time to hatch, just like modern birds.

The largest known dinosaur eggs belonged to ***Hypselosaurus priscus***. These massive eggs measured **12 inches** (30 cm) in length and had a diameter of **10 inches** (25.5 cm) – bigger than a football!

It's always been assumed that all dinosaurs laid eggs with a thick, hard shell. However, new research has shown that early dinosaur eggs laid soft, leathery shells, like today's turtles do.

EGGS-CEPTIONAL FINDS!

One of the largest dinosaur hatcheries has recently been discovered in Narmada Valley, India. Teams of paleontologists have uncovered **92** nesting sites, containing **250** fossilized eggs of the largest known dinosaur – ***Titanosaurus***.

30 years ago, a huge dinosaur rookery, containing more than **300,000** dinosaur eggs, was discovered in the Southern Pyrenees. A team of Spanish and French researchers found huge numbers of egg-shell fragments, complete eggs, and tiny dinosaur bones in mountains that were once an ancient seashore.

Did some dinosaurs incubate, or sit on, their eggs like modern birds? That's the question that has often baffled scientists.

In 1995, the mystery was solved when an emu-sized ***Oviraptor*** dinosaur fossil was discovered in Mongolia. This specimen, nicknamed "Big Mama," was curled up on its nest, protecting a clutch of eggs.

The "Prehistoric Parent Award" goes to the duck-billed ***Maiasaura***, meaning "good mother lizard." Fossil evidence suggests that after hatching, baby ***Maiasaura*** remained in their nest where they were cared for and fed by a parent. These dinosaurs grew quickly and reached their adult size of **20 feet** (6 m) (three times the height of a door) by the age of eight!

NEXTDOOR NEIGHBORS

Dinosaurs weren't the only animals stomping around the prehistoric planet. Let's explore some of the weird and wonderful creatures that lived alongside them.

First, let's head back **300 million** years before the dinosaurs came along. You'd be amazed (and horrified) to meet a selection of supersized insects.

Can you picture the ***Meganeura monyi***: a dragonfly with a **30-inch** (75 cm) wingspan?

Wriggling on the forest floor could be a millipede **8 feet** (2.5 m) long called ***Arthropleura armata*** – that's the equivalent of **four** dachshunds in a row.

Or maybe you'd prefer to come face-to-face with ***Pulmonoscorpius***, one of the largest scorpions to have ever lived. This supersized specimen grew to an impressive length of **28 inches** (70 cm)– just imagine **five** smartphones laid end-to-end.

WHAT'S THE BUZZ?

Bees evolved from predatory wasps who lived **120 million** years ago during the Cretaceous period. Fossils preserved in a fossilized tree resin called **amber** allow us to study ancient bees, with the oldest specimen being **100 million** years old.

Fossil finds have uncovered a collection of small mammals that lived alongside the dinosaurs.

Look up! It's a ***Volaticotherium***. This flying mammal, **5.5 inches** (14 cm) long, could glide through prehistoric forests with a wing-like skin membrane stretching between its body and limbs.

The earliest known mammal is the shrew-like ***Morganucodon***, **4 inches** (10 cm) long, which evolved around **210 million** years ago. It's thought that it laid small, leathery eggs and lived on a diet of beetles and other insects.

From the early Jurassic, around **196 million** years ago, comes the ***Kayentatherium***: a plant-eating mammal about the size of a cat. Fossils have shown that this creature gave birth to litters as large as **38** babies – over **double** the size of modern mammal litters.

Litovoi was a rat-sized mammal that survived the dinosaur wipe-out, but became extinct around **35 million** years ago. It does have one claim to fame: it had one of the smallest brain to body ratios (meaning it had a tiny brain compared to the size of its body) of any other mammal!

Pterosaurs were ancient flying reptiles that soared through the skies during prehistoric times. Let's take a closer look at some of the stand-out specimens.

One of the earliest known pterosaurs is ***Dimorphodon***. This vulture-sized creature had a **5.6-foot** (1.7 m) wingspan, a long tail for balance and supersharp claws.

Its oversized head was lightened with large air-filled openings in its skull.

Ornithocheirus had a **20-foot** (6 m) wingspan.

This pterosaur had a bony crest, or "keel," on the end of its snout. This could have been used to crack open crustacean shells, attract a mate, or to scare off rival pterosaurs.

The seagull-sized ***Rhamphorhynchus*** had **34** needlelike teeth to snatch fish and insects.

They would throw the catch from their teeth into an internal throat pouch, which scientists believe was used for food storage.

The largest ever flying animal was ***Quetzalcoatlus northropi***. With a wingspan the width of a fighter jet, this jumbo pterosaur would leap **8 feet** (2.5 m) into the air to clear the ground for take-off. How high can you jump?

Quetzalcoatlus had a chopstick-like beak, so it's thought that it ate like a heron, snatching fish and reptiles from the water and swallowing them whole.

Let's take a deep dive and reveal the prehistoric predatory creatures that hid in the ocean depths.

Ichthyosaurs first appeared around **250 million** years ago and survived into the late Cretaceous period.

These marine reptiles were one of the largest animals to have ever lived, measuring more than **65 feet** (20 m) long and weighing around **80 tons** (72 mt).

That's **nine times** heavier than a *Tyrannosaurus rex*!

The ***plesiosaur*** was a streamlined marine reptile that swam in the warm seas around **215 million** years ago, hunting squid, fish, and clams.

Its neck took over half its **45-foot-long** (13 m) body, and featured **76** bones, or vertebrae. Humans only have **seven**.

Its cousin, the ***pliosaur***, had a shorter neck but made up for it with a massive head **10 feet** (3 m) long.

This ferocious predator was **three times** longer than a great white shark and weighed as much as **28** of them! It could reach speeds of up to **6 miles per hour** (10 km), using flippers to propel through water.

Deinosuchus is an extinct reptile closely related to crocodiles and alligators. Its name means "terrible crocodile," and for good reason – the largest specimen ever found was almost **40 feet** (12 m) long and had **30** sharp teeth, each the length of an adult thumb!

Sea turtles are one of the oldest creatures on Earth. ***Archelon*** was an extinct marine turtle and is believed to be the largest turtle known, measuring **15 feet** (4.6 m) from head to tail. In comparison, today's leatherback turtle can grow up to **6.5 feet** (2 m) long.

END OF AN ERA

As with any event that happened millions of years ago, it is impossible to be **100%** certain about every detail. One thing we do know for sure, however, is that dinosaurs are now extinct. So how exactly did their disappearance come about?

66 million years ago, an asteroid **6-9 miles** (10-15 km) wide hit Earth. This devastating collision created a colossal crater, with a **90-mile** (150 km) diameter. The asteroid is buried on the seabed off the Mexican coast, and is exactly the same age as the extinction of non-bird dinosaurs.

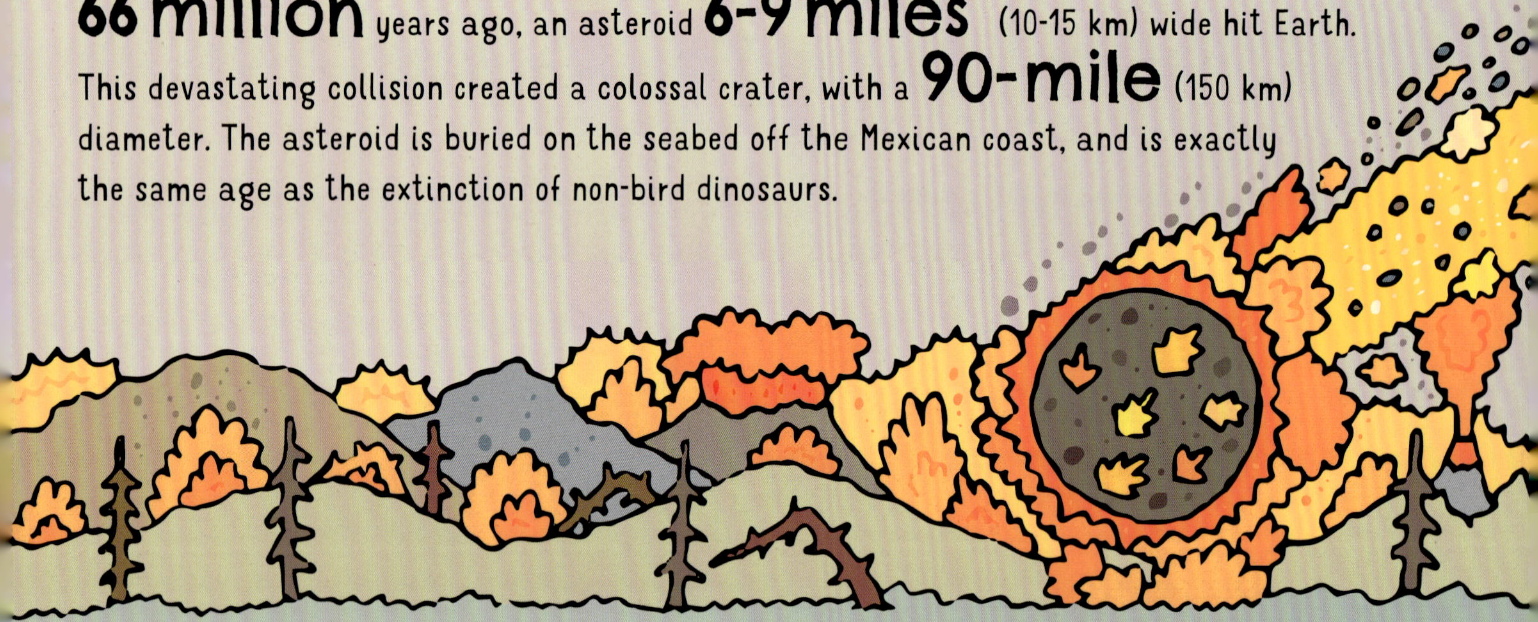

This impact caused a significant amount of debris to be thrown up into the atmosphere, blocking out sunlight and diminishing plant growth. As a result, herbivorous dinosaurs struggled to find food while carnivorous dinosaurs had no prey left to hunt.

Interestingly, research has suggested that if the asteroid had hit Earth just a few minutes later then some dinosaurs might still be around today. The asteroid would have crashed into the deep ocean, causing less debris to rise up and block out the sun's rays.

Despite these catastrophic events, some creatures were able to survive and adapt to a brand new ecosystem.

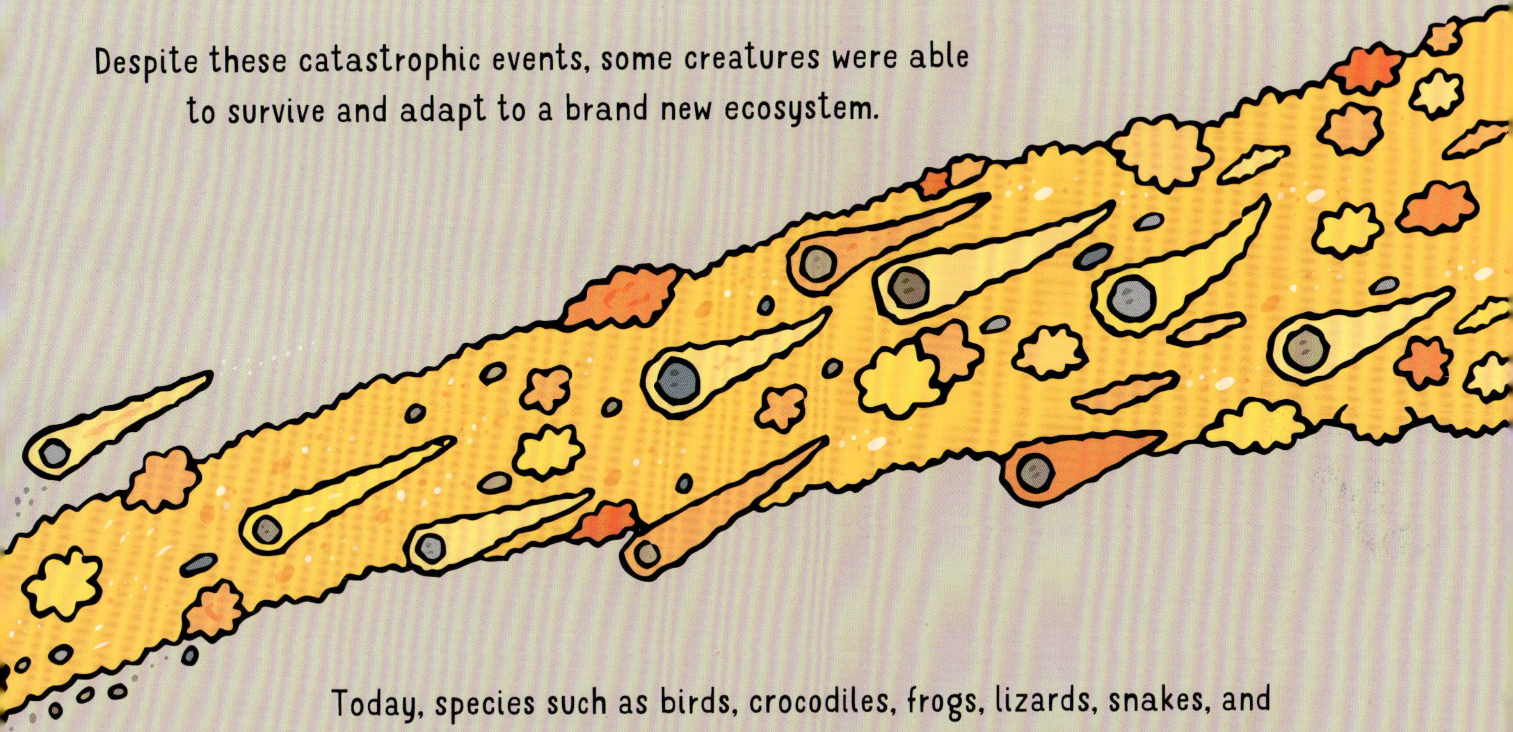

Today, species such as birds, crocodiles, frogs, lizards, snakes, and turtles can all be considered members of the "Survivors' Club." The next group to dominate Earth was on its way ...

Here come the **mammals** (and that includes you!).

So, how do we know so much about these incredible ancient creatures? Paleontologists can explore life from **millions** of years ago by studying fossils.

TRACE FOSSILS:

- **Footprints**
  (The largest of which were the series of herbivore prints discovered in Australia, **5.5 feet** (1.7 m) wide)
- **Skin impressions**
- **Eggs**
- **Coprolites**

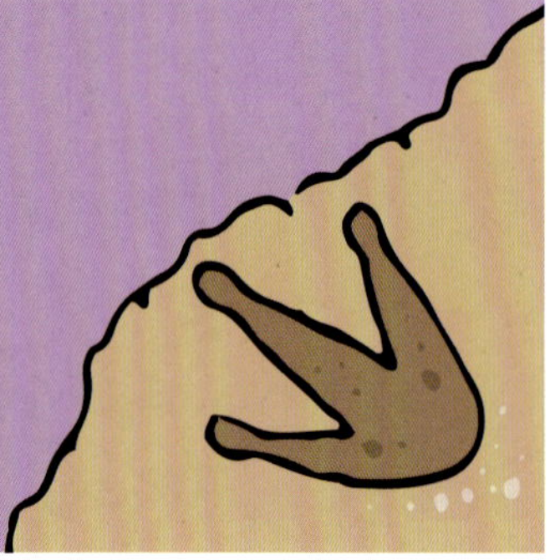

BODY FOSSILS:

- **Teeth**
- **Skulls**
- **Bones**

HERE'S HOW A FOSSIL IS FORMED:

1. When an animal dies, its soft tissue decomposes and only the hard parts, like the skeleton, remain.

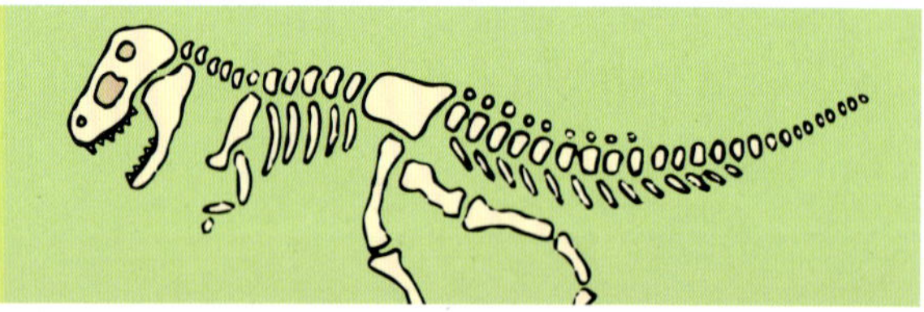

2. The skeleton gets buried by layers of tiny rock particles, called sediment.

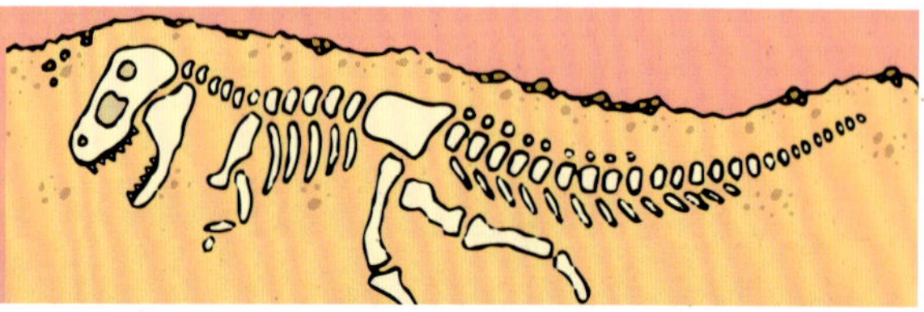

3. More layers build up and, over time, the pressure from the layers turns the sediment into rock.

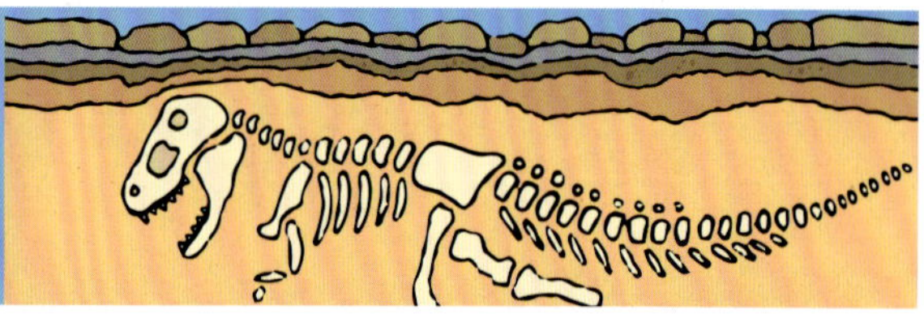

4. Water seeps through the rock, depositing minerals that replaces the bone material, and makes a "rock replica" of the original skeleton.

   This is called a fossil.

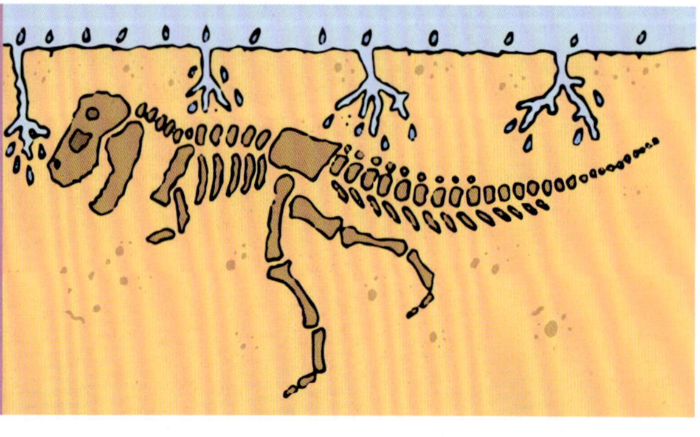

Dinosaur remains have been found in every continent on Earth, including Antarctica. Here are some "Find-a-fossil-hot-spots":

Western North America

This region is home to the first discoveries of ***Stegosaurus*** and ***Brontosaurus***. Over **90** different dinosaur species have been found in just one national park alone: Big Bend National Park in Texas!

China

Recent finds have included the feathered ***Sinosauropteryx***, which has enabled paleontologists to take another look at the evolution of dinosaurs and birds. **4,300** dinosaur footprints were discovered in Zhangjiakou, China. From these paleontologists can figure out the dinosaur's length, weight and speed.

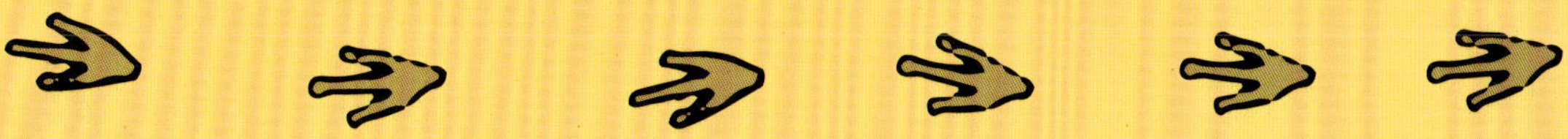

Argentina

One of the most recent finds has been the gigantic ***Chucarosaurus diripienda***, weighing in at **55 tons** (50 mt) and reaching the same length as a blue whale. This specimen's bones were so big that the van carrying the remains back to the laboratory tipped over! (The bones remained in one piece, but the road was damaged!)

TWO BRAINS!

When ***Stegosaurus*** was first discovered almost **150** years ago, paleontologists struggled to believe that such a huge creature came equipped with bird-sized brains.

It was suggested that the ***stegosaurus*** had a **second** brain near its bottom, which was used to control its tail!

DINO DICTIONARY

Check out these helpful words from this book, which you could use when writing about your favorite prehistoric creatures!

Ammonite
Sea creature with a coiled external shell

Angiosperm
A flowering plant

Ankylosaurs
A group of armored dinosaurs

Apex predator
A creature at the top of the food chain, without a natural predator of its own

Asteroid
A small rocky object that orbits the sun

Carnivore
An animal that feeds on other animals

Coprolite
The fossilized poo from ancient creatures

Dinosaur
An ancient reptile. The word means “terrible lizard”

Ecosystem
The interaction of all living things with their environment

Extinction
The dying out or disappearance of a species from Earth

Fossil
The remains or impression of a prehistoric plant or animal, embedded in rock

Gastrolith
A small stone swallowed by some birds, reptiles, and fish to help digestion

Herbivore
An animal that feeds on plants

Incubate
When a creature sits on their eggs to keep them warm before they hatch

Omnivore
An animal that feeds on both plants and animals

Ornithischians
Dinosaurs with a hip structure similar to birds

Paleontology
The study of prehistoric life

Pangea
An ancient supercontinent made up of all Earth's landmass

Panthalassa
The vast superocean that surrounded Pangea

Pterosaur
A prehistoric flying reptile

Saurischians
Dinosaurs with a hip structure similar to reptiles

QUIZ-O-SAURUS

Are you ready for the Dinosaur Quiz?

The answers are at the bottom – but no peeping!

1. When did the dinosaurs first appear on Earth?

A. 145 million years ago

B. 245 million years ago

C. 345 million years ago

2. What does the word "dinosaur" mean?

A. Rotten reptile

B. Colossal creature

C. Terrible lizard

3. An herbivorous dinosaur ate plants. What did a carnivorous dinosaur eat?

A. Other animals

B. Plants and other animals

C. Fruit

4. How long was *Stegosaurus*?

A. 6.2 ft B. 29.5 ft C. 7.5 in

5. How many teeth did *Giganotosaurus* have?

A. 56 B. 36 C. 76

6. Where was *Velociraptor* discovered?

A. Mongolia B. Madagascar C. Morocco

7. How much did an *Argentinosaurus* poo every day?

A. 8.8 lb (around 22 bananas)

B. 88.2 lb (imagine 28 coconuts)

C. 882 lb (the same as 60 watermelons)

8. Which dinosaur's name means "good mother lizard"?

A. *Megalosaurus*

B. *Microraptor*

C. *Maiasaura*

9. How wide was the wingspan of the prehistoric *Meganeura monyi* dragonfly?

A. 30 in B. 3 in C. 246 ft

10. Which supersized prehistoric sea creature was 65 feet long?

A. *Deinosuchus*

B. *Ichthyosaur*

C. *Archelon*

11. How big was the asteroid that collided with Earth 66 million years ago?

A. 3-6 mi wide

B. 6-9 mi wide

C. 12.5-18 mi wide

12. Which of the following are trace fossils?

A. Coprolites B. Teeth C. Footprints

Answers: 1. B. **2.** C. **3.** A. **4.** B. **5.** C. **6.** A. **7.** C. **8.** C. **9.** A. **10.** B. **11.** B. **12.** A and C